Wow, the Wind!

Written by Marie Hardy

The Go Jetters landed Jet Pad.

The Grimbots nodded.

Fun Fact 1!
Wind can help us.

This windmill turns grain into food.

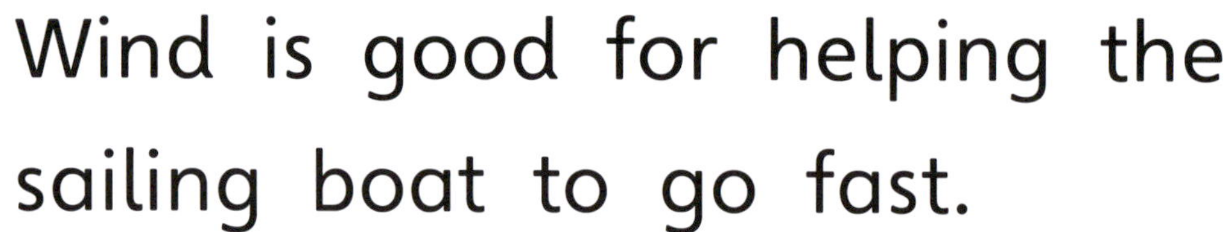

Wind is good for helping the sailing boat to go fast.

A bit of wind can help to cool us down when we feel hot.

7

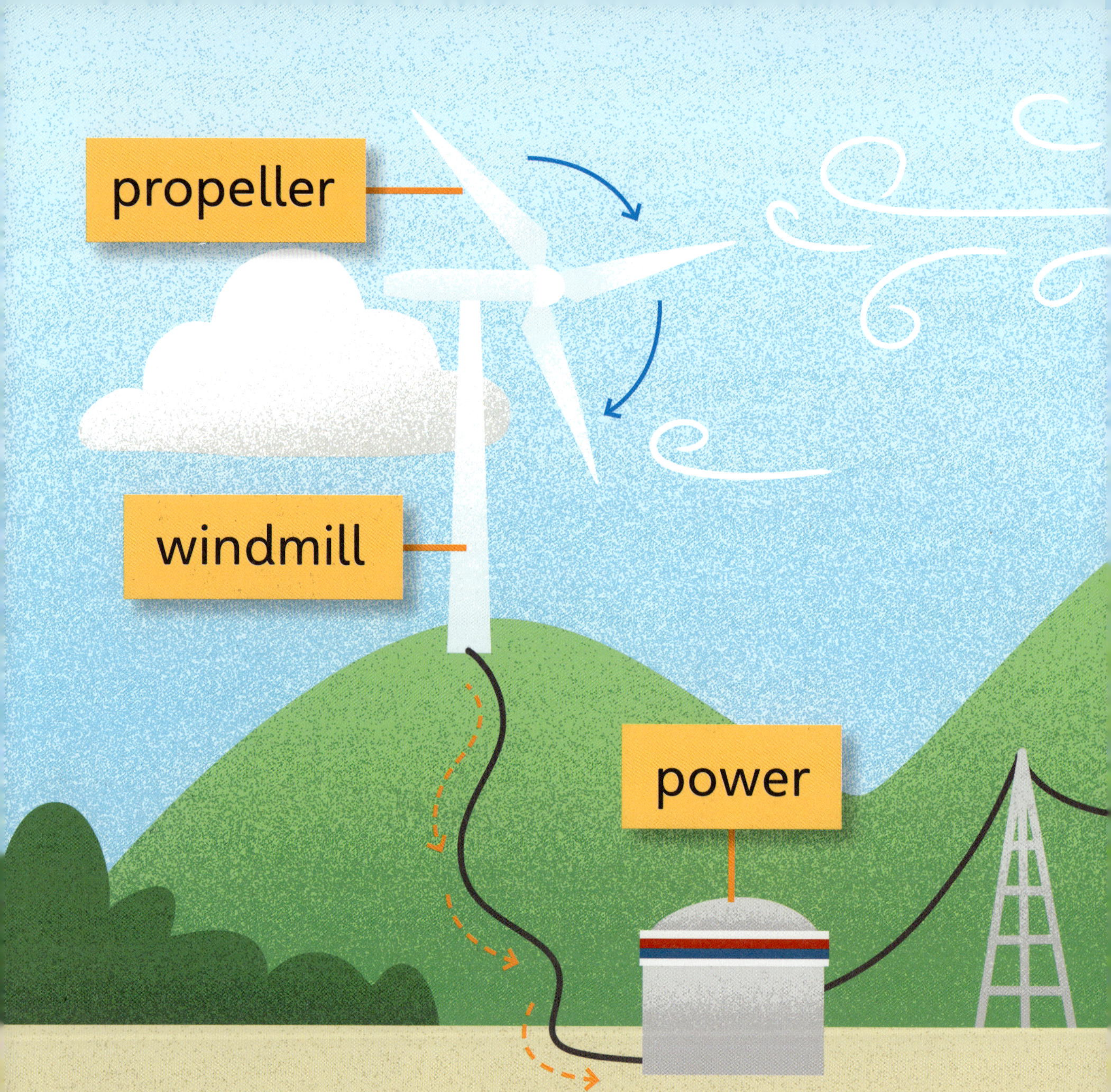

This modern windmill sits on a high tower. The strong wind turns the propellers so that they spin.

Power is collected when the windmill turns. The power is then sent to plug sockets.

10

A big strong wind can uproot trees and block roads.

Fun Fact 3!

When wind and
rain mix, there
might be hail.

Ow!

The rain cools and it gets hard. This is hail.

Big hail can dent a car or harm crops.

Wind power can be much stronger than it seems.

Glitch is in a fix!

The Go Jetters went to help
him. Wind power was good for
Click On power too!